YORK NOTE

General Editors: Professor A
of Stirling) & Professor Suheil Busnrui (*American
University of Beirut*)

Shelagh Delaney

A TASTE OF HONEY

Notes by Loreto Todd
MA (BELFAST) MA PH D (LEEDS)
Reader in International English, University of Leeds

LONGMAN
YORK PRESS

YORK PRESS
Immeuble Esseily, Place Riad Solh, Beirut.

LONGMAN GROUP UK LIMITED
Longman House, Burnt Mill, Harlow,
Essex CM20 2JE, England
Associated companies, branches and representatives
throughout the world

First published in 1992

ISBN 0-582-09644-8

Phototypeset by Gem Graphics, Trenance, Mawgan Porth, Cornwall
Printed in Hong Kong
WC/01

Contents

Part 1

Introduction

Britain in the 1950s

The Second World War ended in 1945, but some of the privations, such as rationing, that were experienced during the war lasted until the early 1950s. Conscription continued and young men had to spend two years serving in the armed forces. Housing, especially in urban areas, was often poor and in short supply, so that many people were forced to live in bedsitters, sharing bathrooms and kitchens. This decade, however, also saw the growth of the Welfare State, the development of television as the major source of entertainment, the emergence of what might be called 'teenage culture' and the beginnings of the affluence and the permissiveness that characterised the 1960s.

It is sometimes hard for young people living in the 1990s to comprehend how different life was in Britain forty years ago, and how controversial were the themes explored in *A Taste of Honey*. Now, one in three marriages ends in divorce; then, the ratio was closer to one in a hundred; single parents were a tiny minority of the population. Now, many young people choose to live together and have children without getting married; then, such behaviour would have been described and condemned as 'living in sin'. Now, approximately one in twenty British citizens is of African, Asian or Caribbean origin; then, apart from long-established Black communities in Bristol, Cardiff, Liverpool and London, the immigration from the Caribbean and the Indian sub-continent had only just begun to increase in scale. Then, male homosexuality was a criminal offence. Not until the Wolfenden Report of 1957 recommended the legalising of private homosexual acts between consenting adults did it become safe for homosexuals to appear in public; now, the kinder term 'gay' is used, and most people reject discrimination in terms of colour, creed or sexual orientation.

In the arts, the 1950s began with a continuation of the conservative work produced in the late 1940s. Then, plays were often written by and for the middle classes. Shaw's *Pygmalion*, for example, under the guise of *My Fair Lady* was one of the biggest stage successes of the 1950s. Then, novels, films and plays tended to have central characters who were either mature or children – teenagers were seldom portayed in a sympathetic way. But changes were taking place. J. D. Salinger's novel *The Catcher in the Rye* (1951) depicted life through the eyes of an unconventional New

York adolescent; and in the cinema, James Dean became famous for his portrayal of the rebellious teenager in *Rebel Without a Cause* (1955). The growth of television had led to the creation of drama for the new medium, and some of these dramas, called soap operas, attempted to address the lives of ordinary working people. The BBC soap opera *The Groves* started in 1954, and *Coronation Street* began its run on independent television shortly after Shelagh Delaney's play was first produced. Although *A Taste of Honey* does not derive from the soap opera, it deals with people from the same place, Salford, and from the same walk of life.

Twentieth-century theatre

There are an estimated one thousand million users of English in the world today, approximately one third of them being native speakers of English. In view of these large numbers, it is not surprising that this century has produced many different kinds of drama, including representations of traditional African and Asian theatre. Limiting ourselves to Britain, we can indicate such different types of drama as:

(*a*) the situation comedies of Oscar Wilde (1854–1900). These were written in the 1890s and dealt with members of the upper middle class. Their plots were often melodramatic and of less significance than the polished wit of the characters. Few playwrights could reproduce Wilde's ultra-sophisticated dialogue, but his plays remained influential. His best-known play is *The Importance of Being Earnest* (1895).

(*b*) the social comedies of George Bernard Shaw (1856–1950). Shaw adopted some of the views of the Norwegian writer, Henrik Ibsen, and tried, by means of wit, humour, and straight talking, to highlight and change social abuses. He dealt with contemporary society and used the device of allowing his characters to address the audience directly. His best-known plays are *Pygmalion* (1914) and *Saint Joan* (1923).

(*c*) the whimsical plays of J. M. Barrie (1860–1937). Barrie exploited and transcended the tradition of sentimental theatre. He is best known for *Peter Pan* (1904) and *Mary Rose* (1920).

(*d*) the poetic drama of W. B. Yeats (1865–1939). Many of Yeats's themes were drawn from Irish mythology and were written in a blank verse form that had not been popular since the seventeenth century. As a playwright, he is perhaps best known for *Deirdre* (1907), *The Death of Cuchulain* (1939) and for his interest in, and enthusiasm for, the stylised, classical Noh drama of Japan. Noh drama seems to have developed no later than the fifteenth century. It used chanting, music, dance and elaborate costumes in its recreation of religious stories and myths.

(*e*) the 'morality' plays of John Galsworthy (1867–1933). Galsworthy dealt with the moral issues involved in industrial disputes, the prison system or the clash between new and old money. He is best known for *Strife* (1909) and *The Skin Game* (1920).

(*f*) the ritualistic drama of T. S. Eliot (1888–1965). Eliot reflected the rituals of the Mass, as well as the use of a chorus, derived from classical Greek theatre, in his dramatisation of the murder of Thomas à Becket in *Murder in the Cathedral* (1935). After the war, he tried to combine drawing-room comedy with religious symbolism. As a playwright, he is also well known for *The Cocktail Party* (1950) and *The Confidential Clerk* (1954).

(*g*) the 'theatre of the absurd' as it was developed by Samuel Beckett (1906–89). Dramatists of the absurd created plays in which normal theatrical conventions were ignored or modified so that life could be represented as meaningless or irrational. The first recognised user of these techniques was the French playwright, Alfred Jarry, but his methods were used and extended in the 1950s and 1960s by Beckett and others. Beckett, in particular, hoped that by exploring the communication and non-communication of characters, language could be made to reveal its in-built deceptions. He is best known for *Waiting for Godot*, first produced in French in 1953, and *Endgame* (1957).

Plays of the 1950s

A useful introductory account of the dramatists who were influential after the war is John Elsom's *Post-War British Theatre* (Routledge and Kegan Paul, London, 1976). Plays did not suddenly become different after the Second World War. They continued to appeal to a minority and tended to be a feature of urban, rather than rural, life. New writers emerged, but Shakespeare, Shaw and, for a time, Eliot, remained popular, and the best guarantee of commercial success was to have a 'star' in the cast. A number of playwrights appeared in the 1950s, however, who might be described as working class, both in terms of their own background and in terms of the language used in their plays. The most significant of these, prior to Shelagh Delaney, were John Osborne and Brendan Behan.

(*a*) John Osborne wrote *Look Back in Anger* (1956). This was perhaps the single most significant play of the decade and heralded an interest in characters who quarrel, often violently, without influencing each other and who tend to be at odds with their society. Kenneth Tynan was almost certainly right when he wrote in *The Observer*:

> I agree that *Look Back in Anger* is a minority taste. What matters, however, is the size of the minority. I estimate it at roughly

6,733,000, which is the number of people in this country between twenty and thirty.

(b) Brendan Behan's play *The Quare Fellow* was staged in East London in May 1956. It is set in an Irish prison in the twenty-four hours before a hanging. The man to be executed, the 'quare fellow', never appears on the stage, and the play focuses on the effect the execution has on the other prisoners. Behan and his play became popular, almost overnight. As Tynan wrote in *The Observer*:

> In Brendan Behan's ... new play ... language is out on a spree, ribald, dauntless and spoiling for a fight ... the tragedy is concealed beneath layer after layer of rough comedy.

The success of, first, Brendan Behan and then Shelagh Delaney can, in part, be accounted for by the talents of Joan Littlewood (b.1924), who produced their plays. She was one of the first directors to create a permanent company, which included a nucleus of writers, producers, musicians, set designers and actors, all working as a team. She and Euan MacColl established the Theatre Workshop in 1945. They toured the country and catered to the interests of mainly working-class people in small towns. In 1953, they took over a music hall, the Theatre Royal, in Stratford in East London, and their productions were commended for their documentary realism, their willingness to tackle serious issues of the time, for their tendency to get audience participation, and for their use of popular music. Among her greatest successes in the 1950s were Behan's two plays, *The Quare Fellow* and *The Hostage* (1958), Shelagh Delaney's *A Taste of Honey* and the Lionel Bart musical, *Fings Ain't Wot They Used To Be*.

The life of Shelagh Delaney

Shelagh Delaney was born in Salford, Lancashire, in 1939, the year when the Second World War broke out. She was educated at Broughton Secondary School but left school to find employment in 1955, when she was sixteen. She worked as a shop assistant and as a cinema usherette but her main interest was in writing. In 1957, when she was eighteen, she sent a copy of her first play, *A Taste of Honey*, to Joan Littlewood. The play opened in the Theatre Royal, East London, in May 1958, and moved to the West End in February 1959. It was produced in New York in 1960 and made into a film in 1962 and has been revived, both in Britain and in the United States, in the 1980s.

Since the late 1950s, Shelagh Delaney has made her living by writing stories, radio, television and theatre plays and screenplays for films such as *Charlie Bubbles* (1968) and *Dance with a Stranger* (1982).

The title and nature of *A Taste of Honey*

The title of the play derives from the the first Book of Samuel in the Bible (chapter 14, verses 24–9 and 43). Jonathan, the son of Saul and friend of David, attacked the Philistines without telling anyone where he was going. While he was away, Saul forbade any of his men to eat before evening. Jonathan, however, did not know about his father's order and when he and his followers found honey:

> . . . he put forth the end of the rod, that was in his hand, and dipped it in an honeycomb, and put his hand to his mouth . . . (verse 27)

When Saul reprimanded his son, Jonathan admitted:

> I did but taste a little honey with the end of the rod that was in my hand, and, lo I must die. (verse 43)

In fact, Jonathan did not have to die then because the people, who loved and admired him, refused to allow him to be punished.

All the characters in the play experience a little pleasure in their 'taste of honey'. Helen and Peter get married, even though their honeymoon period is short. Jo and the Boyfriend share a short interlude of joy over Christmas. Jo and Geof learn to accept the little periods of peace and understanding that they find. But, like Jonathan, the main characters, Jo, Helen and Geof, have to pay for their transitory pleasure. And Jo, who has perhaps found more happiness than the other characters, must pay most.

A note on the text

The text used here is the new edition published by Methuen in 1959, after the play had been revised and modified for the stage. The original play does not differ fundamentally from the text of 1959, but there are two interesting changes. First, the original Peter was sophisticated, suave and kind. He stayed with Helen and offered a home to Jo and the baby. In the modified version, he is a seedy, unattractive and a much less sentimental character. The second major change relates to the ending of the play. Originally, Helen was in the flat when Jo went to the hospital to have her baby. She intended to take Jo and the baby to live with her, leaving Geof alone and with no definite purpose in life. The altered ending is more pessimistic, even though the curtain comes down on Jo smiling and singing. The text is now published, with a commentary and notes, in Methuen Student Editions, first published 1982, reprinted 1990.

Part 2

Summaries
of A TASTE OF HONEY

A general summary

A Taste of Honey spans two acts, each containing two scenes. All the action takes place around the same set, a shabby, uncomfortable flat in a lodging-house in a poor part of Manchester. As well as the five characters – Jo, Helen, Peter, the Boy and Geof – there is a jazz trio in the cast, so that music can be used as an extension to the dialogue and as a means of changing the time and defining the relationships between characters.

Act I, Scene 1 opens with jazz music playing as Helen and her teenage daughter, Jo, move into the flat. From the opening words of the play:

HELEN: Well! This is the place.
JO: And I don't like it.

the focus is on the women, their uneasy relationship, their problems and their attempts to cope with life. To begin with, the women share the attention of the audience, but, as the play progresses, Jo becomes increasingly central to the action. The conversation between Jo and Helen is a kind of verbal sparring, and it soon becomes clear that their relationship is one of ill-concealed hostility.

Jo makes some efforts to improve their dismal surroundings by covering a bare light bulb with a scarf and by planning to create a window box, but Helen's response to such efforts is either semi-humorous:

Everything in it's falling apart, it's true, and there's no heating, but there's a lovely view of the gasworks . . .

or fatalistic:

JO: They're supposed to be left in a cool, dark place.
HELEN: That's where we all end up sooner or later.

Jo accuses her mother of being indifferent to her and of running away from problems. Her accusations seem justified, but she herself is not immune to the same weaknesses.

Before they have unpacked, Peter, the man that Helen has left, walks into the flat, and the three of them indulge in hostile repartee. Peter is surprised that Helen has a daughter, and Jo responds to his lack of interest in her by attempting to sabotage his relationship with her mother. Peter leaves, and the scene ends with Jo describing her fear of the 'darkness inside houses', a theme that is picked up again at the beginning of the second scene.

The first part of Act I, Scene 2 is ostensibly a romantic interlude. We meet Jo's boyfriend, a black youth who is doing his National Service in the navy and whose name is not given until the end of the play. He asks Jo to marry him. They are alone in the flat because Helen has gone away with Peter. The conversation between them reveals that their relationship is based on banter and flirtation, rather than knowledge or deep affection. His sexual interest in Jo is overt but his attitude is casual, and Jo's claim that she loves him is unsupported by the dialogue. The second part of this scene also involves courtship. Helen returns and tells Jo that she is leaving to marry Peter. When Peter comes to collect Helen, the hostile interchanges between him and Jo are resumed. Helen and Peter leave, and Jo, feeling lonely and abandoned, willingly acquiesces to the boy's advances. Helen reappears briefly before leaving finally to get married. Helen's willingness to run away and abandon any inconvenient relationship is beginning to look like a pattern.

In Act II, Scene 1, Jo is pregnant by her black boyfriend, and shares the flat with Geof, a young homosexual who has taken on the role of caring for and protecting Jo. They have a kindly relationship, with humorous banter and little or no hostility. This is the happiest phase of the play, in spite of their poverty and their personal problems. Geof, in his anxiety for Jo's welfare, is responsible for reintroducing Helen into her daughter's life. Helen visits Jo and is both critical of and hostile towards Geof. Peter, who follows her, is even more unpleasant, seeming to enjoy insulting Geof and Jo. Helen and Peter leave, and all the young people have gained from the visit is a cigarette.

In Act II, Scene 2, some months have passed, and Jo is heavily pregnant. She and Geof continue their non-physical partnership, with Geof making efforts to improve the flat, and Jo waiting for the birth of her child. Geof tries to help her by buying her a baby doll, so that she can become accustomed to the way to treat her own baby when it arrives, but it is a white, not a black, doll and triggers off an emotional outburst from Jo. She insists that she does not want the baby, that she will kill it when it is born, or leave it, and, although this is the only act of hostility towards the unborn child, it suggests that Jo is not as different from Helen as she might like to be. Helen returns to the flat, having left Peter, who was paying attention to a younger woman. She drives Geof out and seems willing to take care of Jo when her labour pains start. The caring attitude disappears when Jo tells her mother that her child's father was black. Helen leaves the flat, ostensibly for a drink, but possibly for good. Jo is left entirely alone, smiling and unaware that Geof will not return.

Detailed summaries

Act I, Scene 1

The opening of the play appeals to the eye and to the ear. We see a run-down, poorly furnished flat and hear the sound of jazz music. The combination of these sights and sounds indicates to the audience that *A Taste of Honey* is a play about poor people, at the lower end of the social ladder, and probably about hardship. Jazz music is associated with black people and with the Blues and, in certain slang usage, the word 'jazz' means 'sexual intercourse'.

The mother and daughter who enter are the main figures in the play, and the relationship between parent and child is established as one of the key issues. Helen, the mother, and Jo, the teenage daughter, are moving in with their luggage. All that they have is contained in a couple of suitcases. Helen's first words, 'Well! This is the place', reveal something of her character. She acts, without considering the possible repercussions on those close to her. Jo, in response, condemns her mother's choice. Her quick and contrasting comment sets the tone for much of the dialogue between Helen and Jo. It is similar to the quick-fire repartee of radio or television comedy, where one person sets up a proposition for the other to knock down. The women's situation, however, is far from comic.

The conversation reveals that the flat is cold, dilapidated and in a bad area. Helen has an appalling cold, and they have little money and no regular employment. Helen supports them by means of 'immoral earnings'. (In view of the fact that this claim is made to the audience by Jo, 'we're supposed to be living off her immoral earnings', it probably means that Helen accepts money from her boyfriends and not that she is a prostitute.) Helen is anxious to have a drink, whereas Jo refuses to have anything to do with alcohol. She disapproves of Helen's drinking and dislikes the taste. In spite of the mother–daughter relationship, Jo addresses her mother as Helen, indicating her lack of respect and her claim to have equal rights. Helen uses a similar technique when she criticises Jo's efforts to find the gas fire. Instead of addressing Jo either by her name or as 'you', she distances her by using the third-person singular 'she' – 'She can never see anything till she falls over it' – and by suggesting that Jo is clumsy. Helen is not the only character who uses 'she' or 'he' when we might expect 'you'. There are many comments of this type in the play, some of which are directed at the audience. Like the music, they link the characters and the audience in a special bond, whilst also signalling the alienation of the speaker from the person referred to in this way.

Helen is indifferent to her surroundings, partly because she has a cold, and partly because she has no instinct to turn the flat into a home. Jo, on the other hand, wants to personalise their surroundings. She drapes a scarf round the bare light bulb and plans to make coffee. Both acts are significant. The scarf may look attractive but could cause a fire. And tea, not coffee, was the usual drink of people like Jo and Helen. Jo's selection of coffee may suggest that she has rising social aspirations. Her attempts to light the gas stove are both dangerous and humorous and perhaps underline her lack of practical experience.

Helen's conversation turns to the subject of a handsome boy she has seen in the building, and she enquires of Jo: 'you've never had a boyfriend, have you?' Jo's reply: 'No. I used to like one of your fancy men, though', reveals the type of life Helen has been leading. When Jo describes the man, she reveals that: 'he ran off with that landlady's daughter.' The sound of a tugboat provokes more comment on the flat. It is close to the river and the slaughterhouse. Helen's method of coping with her surroundings is to make semi-humorous, detached comments:

> The slaughterhouse. Where the cows, sheep and pigs go in and all the beef, pork and mutton comes out.

Jo's response to the squalor is to unpack some flower bulbs, which she plans to grow in a window box. It emerges that she has stolen the bulbs from the Park, but Helen's comment is merely to say casually: 'That's the way to do things.' Equally casual is her comment that Jo will have: 'a shocking journey to school each day . . . It must be miles and miles.' As we learn from this and subsequent comments, Helen has shown little interest in Jo's education, moving her from school to school, and is quite content that she should leave school at Christmas, without qualifications and with few prospects. Instead of discussing Jo's future, Helen reminisces about her own first job 'in a tatty little pub' and sings a song that has many sentimental elements, such as 'song birds', 'woods', 'sunset', 'old folks' and a 'baby' on the 'knee'. A closer look at the song, however, suggests that it is a relatively cruel parody of a sentimental ballad. The birds are returned to the 'wild' woods, where they are not safe; the sunset is given to 'the blind', who cannot see it; and the old folks are given a memory only of the child they once nurtured. Helen uses the song to daydream about the future she might have had, if she had taken up singing. The theme of lost opportunities is continued when she refuses to interfere in Jo's decisions, reminding her: 'it's your life, ruin it your own way', and she agrees with Jo when she says that Helen was an expert at ruining lives, telling her to: 'give praise where praise is due, I always say. I certainly supervised my own downfall.'

Helen changes the subject to a dream Jo has had, but Jo does not immediately remember what Helen is talking about, as she mentioned the dream in passing, and Helen did not appear to be listening to her. This shows that Helen is very alert, picking up on things when she appears to have missed them. Jo describes the dream, in which Helen's dead body is found under a rosebush. If Jo expects to shock or upset her mother with her ghoulish description, the tactic fails because Helen agrees that 'we should be used for manure when we're gone', and urges Jo to make her a cup of coffee.

While Jo is making the coffee, Helen rummages in the suitcase and finds some of her daughter's drawings. Showing more interest than usual, perhaps because of her own reverie about being a singer, Helen asks Jo if she has ever thought of going to an art school, and even offers to pay for her tuition. In spite of her youth, Jo insists that it is too late and seems almost to enjoy the prospect of wasting her talent as long as she can blame her mother for the waste.

Jo asks Helen why they left their previous accommodation, and challenges Helen's explanation that she was fed up with the last place. Shrewdly, Jo suspects that her mother is running away from someone, and Helen is angered by Jo's suspicions. Perhaps to avoid the 'bloody good hiding' that Helen threatens, Jo decides to look for the bathroom to take a bath, but, before she can take it, Peter, a car salesman, walks in. He is obviously the man that Helen has run away from. She is startled and somewhat annoyed that he has discovered her whereabouts. In spite of the close relationship that seems to have existed between Helen and Peter, he is surprised to discover that she has a daughter. His comment is a cold, third-person assessment: 'That puts another ten years on her', which draws a covert comparison between Helen and a second-hand car with 'x' number of miles on the clock.

Jo takes every opportunity to obstruct the relationship between Peter and Helen. Peter dismisses Jo as 'a snotty-nosed daughter' and is determined to win back Helen, reminding her that she cannot afford to lose a man like him. He jokingly asks Helen to marry him, and when she replies: 'I'm old enough to be your mother', he insists that he is partial to the 'mother and son relationship'. Helen extends the parent–child theme by telling Peter that he liberates something in her which is not her 'maternal instincts'. There is clearly a strong physical attraction between them.

Peter and Helen indulge in some coarse humour and he sings snatches from popular songs while Jo makes coffee that neither Helen nor Peter can drink. He continues to flirt with Helen and suggests that Jo is old enough to look after herself. Eventually, Helen gets rid of him and prepares to go to bed.

In the closing stages of the scene, the talk between Helen and Jo is of darkness and death. Helen loves the darkness of which Jo is afraid. Jo maintains that she is not frightened by all darkness, but only by 'the darkness inside houses'. The scene ends with Helen asking Jo how she would react if she, Helen, got married again. Jo answers that she would have her mother locked up in an institution, and, on this comment, the lights and the music fade.

NOTES AND GLOSSARY:

The notes are meant to draw your attention to points in the text that you may have missed or misunderstood.

a comfortless flat in Manchester: Shelagh Delaney does not provide as many stage directions as do other playwrights such as Sean O'Casey or Harold Pinter, but those that she does provide are intended to be significant. This description indicates that the play will have a northern, urban setting, a setting poorer than that of the television soap opera *Coronation Street*, where the characters live in their own houses

***Jazz music*:** the theme of colour becomes increasingly marked in the course of the play. The jazz music, with its strong black associations, is like a subconscious undercurrent of tension

***a semi-whore*:** this is an unusual description and, in part, conditions the reader's response to Helen. It would be interesting to compare the reaction to Helen by a reader and by a member of an audience who was not aware of the description. The word 'semi-whore' suggests that Helen takes money from the men she has lived with, but she does not seem to be a prostitute. It is possible that she is being pushed into prostitution by Peter, and Jo's claim that they are living off Helen's 'immoral earnings' might support this view

I don't owe you a thing: Jo asserts her independence early in the play. Shortly after this, she calls her mother 'Helen', again stressing that she is not tied to her mother by bonds of affection or respect

Others may pray for their daily bread: Helen's interest in alcohol is one of the first things we learn about her. Her packing has been hasty and poorly structured, but she has been careful to carry her whisky in a carrier bag and the glasses in her handbag 'for safety'. She occasionally uses biblical references. This one refers to the Lord's Prayer: 'Give us this day our daily bread'

get it down you: drink it

shilling in the slot: a shilling was equivalent to 5p. It was put into a gas meter to buy a certain amount of gas

You're knocking it back worse than ever: you're drinking more heavily than ever before. Helen agrees that she is drinking more, reinforcing the suggestion that she is only just on the edge of respectability

Mind you don't gas yourself: Jo does not seem to be used to dealing with gas stoves and has to be reminded to be careful. This suggests her youth and inexperience

one of your fancy men: one of your lovers. Jo may be young but she has considerable knowledge of the seamier side of life, and talks to her mother as to an equal, or an inferior

he ran off with that landlady's daughter: this is the first reference in the play to someone running off; the idea of running away from problems becomes thematic in the play

It wasn't his nose I was interested in: Helen enjoys coarse, earthy humour and does not think of protecting her daughter from it

Eee, there's a terrible draught: this use of 'Eee' is the first clear example we have had of a quintessentially Lancashire usage

It's self all the time: Helen complains that Jo shows her no consideration and thinks only of herself

That's where we all end up: Helen is aware of the shortness of life and is determined to have as good a time as she can. She accepts the limitations of her position. Jo, on the other hand, is unwilling to accept things as they are. She wants to improve her surroundings by planting bulbs. Her own amorality is indicated by the fact that she has stolen the bulbs from the park

into the middle of next week: Helen is using a cliché to tell Jo that if she, Helen, had spoken as rudely to her mother, she would have been knocked unconscious

Very wise too: Helen is not a possessive mother. When Jo tells her that she plans to get away as soon as she has earned some money, she is commended for her good sense

you're not very fond of work: Helen's comment and Jo's rejoinder that she takes after her mother in not liking work seem to have an element of truth in them. Helen doesn't have a regular job, although, in the 1950s, there was almost full employment. And, although Jo talks about work, she does not actually get a job. Perhaps they are more alike than either of them would care to admit

I'd give the song birds: parodies of sentimental ballads were not uncommon in the 1950s when singers like Stan Freeberg, for example, had hits by changing 'I believe for every drop of rain that falls/A flower grows' into 'I believe for every drop of rain that falls/Someone gets wet'

It's a waste of time interfering with other people: Helen's fatalism is understandable, but it could be an excuse for not getting involved in helping Jo to organise her future

I'm not getting married like you did: Jo's intended criticism of her mother's rash marriage turns out to be prophetic

we all end up same way: this is another example of northern usage. Standard English speakers would prefer 'the same way'. Helen's pessimism and her awareness that we all end up dead is almost like her signature tune

under a rosebush: children are sometimes told that babies are found under gooseberry bushes or rose bushes

She wouldn't think . . . at that age: Helen frequently refers to Jo's age, suggesting that she is going through an awkward, adolescent phase, and Jo herself says that she is 'nearly eighteen'

It's the gipsy in me: this is a quotation from a popular song, but it also indicates that Helen is not willing to take responsibility for her actions. She may have ruined Jo's prospects by moving her from school to school, but she does not see this as her fault

I'm not just talented, I'm geniused: Jo thinks highly of herself. She certainly feels she has the right to set herself up in judgment of her mother. But knowing she is talented does not encourage her to exploit her abilities. Like her mother, she is content to drift

I'll pay: Helen tries to encourage Jo to go to art school and even offers to pay the fees. Jo is almost determined to be a martyr, insisting that it is too late for her to go to art school

You'll find the communal latrine and wash-house: Helen's joking reference to the bathroom hides the squalor of their surroundings where, as Helen put it earlier, 'we share a bathroom with the community'

Look what the wind's blown in: Helen's remark is a version of the common phrase 'look what the cat's dragged in'

Did you think you could escape me, dear?: Peter clearly has a hold over Helen. His endearments 'dear' and, later, 'kid' and 'darling' are almost a way of avoiding using Helen's name. When we first meet Peter, it seems as if he is possibly a pimp, that is, a man who lives off the 'immoral earnings' of women

What's this one called?: Jo's question suggests that Peter Smith is only one in a long line of Helen's boyfriends

make yourself scarce: Helen's insistence that Jo should get out of the way while she is talking to Peter gives us a glimpse of the rejection that Jo has had to put up with in the past, and may explain her rudeness towards her mother

Get rid of her: Peter's reaction to Jo is that she is a nuisance to be got rid of. He describes her as 'snotty-nosed', says he had not 'bargained' on Helen having a daughter, wants Helen to 'Send her to the pictures', and claims that 'she's old enough to take care of herself'

I told you I was throwing my hand in: this is ambiguous, perhaps suggesting that Helen worked for Peter as a prostitute

You can't afford to lose a man like me: Peter's statement is ambiguous. He could simply mean that he has money and so is worth knowing. He could also mean that he has been instrumental in putting money Helen's way. It is interesting that he says 'a man like me' instead of just 'me', perhaps again suggesting that he is a pimp, a suggestion reinforced by his telling Helen, 'You can't renege on the old firm', meaning, 'You can't go back on your contract'

I'll make an honest woman of you: I'll marry you

If you ask me again I might accept: in spite of her flippancy, Helen may still want the security that marriage could offer her

Can't bear to see me being affectionate with anybody: Helen suggests that Jo might be jealous of Peter, but her idea of showing 'affection' is much less restrained than the phrase might suggest

I should have thought their courtship had passed the stage of symbolism: Jo's remark to the audience is much more formal than we might have expected from a girl who has had such a poor education

rolled on the thigh of a coal black mammy: Peter's humour is coarse, racist and full of sexual innuendo

a slouch: someone who is incompetent; in this case, at attracting men

the cat's been on the strawberries: this is not a well-known expression. It is an insult, addressed to Helen. A 'cat' was a prostitute and 'strawberries' were pimples caused by alcohol abuse

I'm not frightened of the darkness outside: Jo's interest in different types of darkness links up with references to darkness in Scene 2

Act I, Scene 2

The theme of darkness with which Act I, Scene 1 ends is picked up in Act I, Scene 2, not only in the reference to the dark evenings of winter but also because Jo's boyfriend is black. The young man, who is not named and who is called the 'Boy', has picked Jo up from school and is walking her home. Jo asserts that she does not care about his colour, an assertion that he takes positively, although it might be a sign of her lack of interest in him. In a conversation which reveals how little they know about each other, we learn that the Boy is on leave from the navy and that Jo is leaving school and getting a part-time job in a bar. He asks her to marry him and then asks her age. Jo says that she is 'nearly eighteen' and agrees to marry him but plans to keep the news from Helen. Her assertion that Helen is not colour prejudiced may be a defence of Helen or it may be wishful thinking. Subsequent events certainly prove it to be untrue.

The Boy has bought Jo a ring which they put on a ribbon and hang round her neck, because it is too big for her and also to conceal it from Helen. Like Helen and Peter, the Boy refers to Jo in the third person – when she wants to play with the toy car he has in his pocket, he says, 'She doesn't even know how it works.' In spite of the gentle banter of their conversation and in spite of their agreement to get married, there is no substantial commitment between the young couple. Instead of planning to see Jo later, he intends to go to the pub with his friends. As he leaves, he sings to the audience, the music providing a transition to the next part of the scene where Helen and Jo are together in the flat.

They chat for a while about Jo's wish to go to the cinema. Again, the tone of their conversation is very frank and open, unexpectedly so for a mother and daughter. Their conversation then turns to the subject of Jo's birth. We learn that Jo's father was not Helen's husband, but a mentally handicapped man she had a brief affair with. When her husband found out that she was pregnant with another man's child, he threw Helen out of their house. She blames Jo for her misfortune, telling her, 'that was your fault', and behaving as unrealistically as Jo had when she blamed Helen for all the problems of her young life. In an unusual exchange, Jo says that under the same circumstances she would behave as Helen's husband had done, but Helen disagrees. Reflecting on life, Helen fatalistically remarks: 'We're all at the steering wheel of our own destiny. Careering along like drunken drivers.' Juxtaposed with this admission of her lack of control over her actions is her revelation that she and Peter are getting married. The implication is that this decision, too, is irresponsible.

Peter arrives to the accompaniment of music shortly after this announcement. Jo criticises her mother's figure, but is greeted with Helen's usual joking attitude to criticism. Helen goes to get changed, and Jo tries to irritate Peter, and then suddenly attacks him physically. Her words are childish, almost accusing Peter of being the attacker: 'You leave me alone. And leave my mother alone too.' Jo tries to annoy Peter further by demanding to see the photographs of his ex-girlfriends that he keeps in his wallet and then commenting rudely on them. The motif of blackness recurs with the discussion of Peter's eye-patch, worn because he has lost an eye.

Jo wants to see the hole under the patch and tries to provoke Peter by asking him if he wears the patch going to bed. Peter remarks crudely that, 'there is one highly recommended way for a young girl to find out', the way in question being to go to bed with him. He begins to sing about love, and Helen, too, can be heard singing off-stage. Helen emerges, having changed; Peter is delighted with her appearance, and he tells her: 'Helen, you look utterly fantastic.' He clowns about with her hat, and as she remonstrates with him and Jo, the age difference between Helen and Peter begins to show. Helen and Peter eventually leave, for an indefinite period, leaving Jo on her own.

As Jo lies on the bed crying, the Boy comes in to the sound of music. He comments on the dirt: 'The children round here are filthy.' They resume their earlier banter, and their lack of commitment to each other is stressed when he admits, 'I'm one on his own', and she replies, 'So am I.' He reminds her that he will soon be gone, but Jo asks him to stay with her for Christmas. Their conversation is full of acknowledgements that he will probably not return, with Jo showing bleak realism in saying: 'I'll probably never see you again', and suggesting that the Boy is 'only after one thing'. Nevertheless, she seems content with the pleasure of the moment.

The wedding bells that mark the transition from this episode to the next are not for Jo but for Helen. Jo has a heavy cold and is not going to Helen's wedding. Helen discovers the ring Jo is wearing and reacts angrily at first, saying 'you silly little bitch'. However, she does try to give Jo advice, showing rare consideration for her daughter's welfare: 'Oh Jo, you're only a kid. Why don't you learn from my mistakes? It takes half your life to learn from your own.' Jo rejects this solicitude, but she does, however, pay Helen a rare and grudging compliment: 'You look marvellous, considering.' Before Helen leaves, Jo asks for more information about her father. Helen replies that he was 'just a bit – retarded.' They part on relatively friendly terms, with Jo wishing Helen good luck.

NOTES AND GLOSSARY:

naval rating: the lowest rank of sailor

I don't know why I love you but I do: first line of a popular love song

I'm leaving Helen: we hear of Jo's plans to leave her mother before we hear of Helen's plans to go off with Peter

Mau-Mau: an independence movement in Kenya in the 1950s

Cardiff: this city, like Bristol, Liverpool and London, has had a black community much longer than non-port cities such as Birmingham or Leeds

Honey: the Boy uses this endearment for Jo. A taste of honey could, by extension, be a taste of Jo

Okay, you're the boss: the Boy never pushes himself on Jo. He frequently defers to her wishes

daft: a northern word for 'silly', 'stupid'. The word is often humorous rather than offensive. In this context it would not give offence, as Jo uses it affectionately. It can, however, also imply 'insane'

I certainly hope it isn't a she … in this state: this is the first oblique reference in the play to homosexuality, and, although it is meant to be humorous, it suggests Helen's prejudice

National Service: two years of compulsory service in the armed forces for all healthy men over the age of eighteen

I Was a Teenage …: there have been several films beginning with this title, including *I Was a Teenage Frankenstein* and *I Was a Teenage Werewolf*. They are low budget, unpretentious entertainment

The Ten Commandments: an epic, biblical film, made in 1956 and starring Charlton Heston

Desire Under the …: *Desire Under the Elms*, a play by Eugene O'Neill which was released as a film in 1958

on't streets: a northernism for 'on the streets', a euphemism for being a prostitute

You might have to do that yet: Helen faces the possibility that Jo might be forced to be a prostitute if she cannot earn money any other way

sling her out: throw her out

dirty little spiv: flashily dressed young man who rarely had regular employment but made money through illegal trading. The racist overtone of this remark contradicts Jo's assurance to the Boy earlier in the scene that Helen was not prejudiced

you're forty years old: Helen does not deny Jo's claim, but Jo may be exaggerating. She is certainly being spiteful when she tells her mother: 'You don't look forty. You look a sort of well-preserved sixty'

glad rags: best clothes, usually attractive

I shan't be a tick: I will only be a short time

there is one highly recommended way for a young girl to find out: Peter is suggesting that the only way she would find this out is by sleeping with him

Do you fancy me?: Jo is not averse to teasing Peter. She seems to want him to be attracted to her

Bang-on: slang for 'absolutely excellent'

moonlight flit: leaving a place without telling anyone and without paying the bills

Lord's Day Observance Society: a group of people, often thought to be over-zealous, who argue that the Christian Sabbath on Sunday should be kept holy

He's got a wallet full of reasons: Helen is unsentimental about Peter. His greatest attraction is that he has money and is willing to spend it on her

a quid: slang for one pound. This was quite a lot of money in the mid-1950s, when the average weekly wage was approximately eight pounds

called to the bar: successful candidates for barristers' examinations are called to the Bar, meaning that they have become qualified. Helen enjoys punning as she compares Jo's part-time job in a public-house or 'bar' to a barrister's

Black Hole of Calcutta: a popular phrase, drawn from colonial history and applied to dark, cramped space. In 1756, the Nawab of Bengal confined 146 British prisoners in a small, dark cell. Only 23 of them survived. The centenary of the event was commemorated by some Indians and is sometimes given as one of the causes of the Indian Mutiny (1857–9). The Mutiny led to the transfer of the administration of India from the British East India Company to the Crown

opium pellet: a drug. In romantic novels, the heroine was sometimes given such a drug so that she would not resist the advances of her ravisher

fancy bit: attractive woman

If she was dressed up like Hope Gardens: if she was overdressed and looked good from a distance. The expression 'dressed up like Hope Gardens' means to look gaudy and cheap

Pirate King: pirates, such as Long John Silver in *Treasure Island*, often wore black eye-patches

You've had your chips: you've missed your opportunity

My heart's broke: this is the first example of non-standard grammar

Woolworths: a department store, popular for its low-priced goods

'gross clasps of the lascivious Moor': unwanted embraces of the passionate black man. This quotation from Shakespeare's *Othello* (1604) shows that the Boy is more educated than he may at first appear

'Oh ill-starred wench': unlucky girl. Desdemona was murdered by Othello

If that's what you want: the Boy is very willing to stay, but, once again, he leaves the decision about how far their relationship should go to Jo

Be sharp: be quick

spends his money like water: spends lavishly as if money were as plentiful as water

knocking about with: going around with

down-and-out boozer: a homeless, unemployed alcoholic

meths: methylated spirits, a form of cheap alcohol used for fuel. It is sometimes drunk by homeless alcoholics

Old Nick: the Devil

It's hereditary, isn't it?: Jo is frightened that her father's mental illness may have been passed on to her, and through her to any child she might have. She does not seem to worry that her mother's weaknesses might also be hereditary

half-wit: offensive term for a person who is mentally retarded

Puritan: member of a strict Protestant sect; person who disapproves cf physical gratification

---

Act II, Scene 1

The opening of Act II, Scene 1 is similar to that of the first scene of the play. There is music to be heard, fairground music rather than jazz, and two figures enter the dark flat. Jo is again one of the figures, but the second one is a young man called Geof. This time, Jo is quite clearly pregnant, but she and Geof appear to be happy together. They have just been enjoying themselves at the fair and have brought a bunch of balloons back to the flat with them.

It soon becomes clear that they have met at the fair and do not know a great deal about each other. Geof comments on the size of the flat and tries to make himself useful, in the hope that Jo will let him stay. Jo knows that he has been thrown out of his lodgings by his landlady, and, although Geof says it was because he did not pay his rent, Jo suspects that it was because the landlady found him entertaining a man.

Jo tries to persuade Geof to tell her what homosexuals 'do', even bribing him with the promise of a comfortable couch. Geof refuses to answer her questions, and when he makes it clear that he intends to leave, Jo apologises and asks him to stay.

While Jo is getting sheets and blankets, Geof sees her drawings and says that they are just like her, having 'no design, rhythm' or 'purpose' to them. He does not like their sentimentality but nevertheless thinks that Jo should go to a decent school, or should, at least, learn some discipline.

Jo refuses to be taken 'in hand' by Geof, suggesting that someone else had tried to help her but that he only stayed with her between Christmas and New Year. Geof questions Jo about whether she liked or loved her boyfriend. Jo replies that she thinks she may have loved him but that she cannot be sure because she has had so little experience of love.

Jo and Geof talk easily and unselfconsciously about her pregnancy. Geof reminds her that she could get an abortion, even though abortions were illegal in Britain at the time, but Jo thinks that it would be 'terrible' to take away the baby's life. They move from discussing Jo's pregnancy to the subject of money, and Jo tells him she only has her wages, which do not last long by the time she has paid for what she needs. Her necessities include 'stockings and make-up and things'. Geoff tries to persuade her that she is too young to need make-up and that she should save her money for the baby, but Jo plans to stop working soon, because she is self-conscious about her pregnancy, and thinks that people are always looking at her. In his anxiety for her welfare, Geof suggests that Jo's mother might help, but Jo is almost superstitious about discussing her baby; she does not want to make plans or think about the future. The conversation shifts to a lighter, almost childish, level, and they talk about their youth and their uniqueness, joke about Jack Spratt and his wife, and Geof recites two rhymes, neither of which is particularly light-hearted. Before they go to sleep, Jo sings a song, called 'Black Boy', and tells Geof that the father of her child is black, although, in her account, she transforms him into an African prince. Geof accepts the information in a totally matter-of-fact way and promises to clean up the flat the following morning. Jo compares him to an elder sister in his efforts to take care of her.

Music is used to indicate that time has passed. It is now a month or two later and Jo is beginning to find her pregnancy irksome. Geof is making a child's gown while Jo comments on the filth of the children in the neighbourhood. Her worry about the mental state of her own child is indicated by her claim that women should not be allowed to bring retarded children into the world. Jo's mood swings from elation, when she feels the child kick, to depression, when she insists that she hates babies. Geof is shouldering most of the responsibilities. He has paid the rent from his grant and asked the landlady to make a wicker basket as a cradle for the baby. He has bought Jo a book, *Looking After Baby*, and seems willing to put up with her teasing and insults. He asks Jo if he is repulsive to her, kisses her and asks her to marry him. Jo admits that she likes him but does not enjoy 'all this panting and grunting'. Geof accepts her refusal but declares that he would rather be dead than away from her. She has given him a purpose in life that he lacked before meeting her.

Helen comes in, and immediately tries to take control. Geof has asked her to come, but he does not want Jo to know that he has interfered. Helen and Jo argue loudly, and when Geof tries to intervene to protect Jo, Helen tells him that they both enjoy rows. They both turn on Geof, Helen insulting his manhood and telling him to leave; Jo insisting he deserves what he gets and ordering him to make a cup of tea. Helen shows that she knows a great deal about having babies, and promises to help Jo financially when she realises that Jo is not receiving any maternity benefit.

Peter comes in, complaining loudly about having been left outside so long in the filthy street. He is in an aggressive state of drunkenness, sings a song that draws attention to Jo's pregnancy, and insults Geof with a variety of abusive names. He also speaks cruelly to and about Helen, referring to her as 'a sour-faced old bitch', and stressing the age difference by suggesting that he is like Oedipus, who married his mother. Their relationship has clearly deteriorated in the intervening months. All they have in common now is their interest in drink. Peter takes back the money Helen has left out for Jo and delights in telling a story about how he picked up two young women on a bus and stayed with them for two weeks. He lurches off to the bathroom, and while he is away Helen and Jo question each other about their relationships. They cannot agree about anything, but Helen offers Jo a room and good food if she will go with her and leave her 'pansified little freak'. Peter returns, complaining about the cockroaches in the bathroom. In front of him, Helen again offers to look after Jo, even though he does not want 'that bloody slut' in his home. Helen seems genuinely distressed that Jo is living in such terrible conditions. She even asks if Jo would like her to stay with her in the flat. Jo says no, and Helen follows Peter out to the pub. The visit has produced nothing but tension and has left Jo and Geof with no extra money, but with the cigarette Helen gave Jo.

NOTES AND GLOSSARY:

maisonette: usually a self-contained flat, occupying two floors and having its own entrance

up the creek: the wrong way

you daft thing: you silly/mad thing. The phrase is often used affectionately in the north of England

under the arches: many homeless people find shelter under the railway arches. This may also be a satirical reference to a popular song: 'Underneath the arches, I dream my dreams away'

people like you: homosexuals. Jo's questioning is aggressive and unwholesome. She is willing to give Geof shelter in return for details of his sexual behaviour

You want taking in hand: this is a northern expression equivalent to 'You need someone to look after and discipline you'

stockings and make-up and things: Jo has little money left to prepare for the baby's arrival when she has bought the items she feels are essential. The fact that she sees these things as essential shows where her priorities lie

Spratts: a well-known manufacturer of biscuits for dogs

Thessaly: a region in Greece. It had a coastline on the Aegean Sea and extensive fertile plains. Many comic verses for children begin with references to exotic places.

Often, the selection is largely for the purposes of rhyme as in: 'There was a young lady from Riga/Who went for a ride on a tiger'. Greece, the source of much western culture, was selected in this rhyme because it produced so many philosophers or 'lovers of wisdom'

Pippin Hill: the word 'pippin' was a general term for several types of eating apple. 'Pippin Hill' was used, especially in Devon and Somerset, for low hills, often favoured as the sites for orchards. Gradually, the association with apples was lost and 'Pippin Hill' became a name for a country district

Lagonda: a make of luxury car

Beggars can't be choosers: a well-known proverb meaning, 'People should be satisfied with the little they have; there is no point aspiring to anything better'

***Black Boy*:** this song and the earlier reference to the baby being born 'dead or daft' show that Jo is thinking constantly about the baby, even though she has told Geof that there is plenty of time to prepare for it

big sister: Jo thanks Geof for his kindness by questioning his masculinity

it's walking away: it's infested with lice

deficient: mentally handicapped

grant: money paid to students as an allowance

as thick as thieves: very friendly

croft: a northern expression for waste ground

black beast: Shakespeare's Othello was referred to as an 'old black ram'. Geof unconsciously echoes the Boy who referred to himself as Othello and to Jo as Desdemona. His remark is also an example of the racist stereotype of the sexual prowess of all black men

Romeo: Helen's remark is an ironic inversion of the cliché about the romantic hero

blew you in: Jo's remark mirrors ironically Helen's comments on Peter's arrival in Act I, Scene 1: 'Look what the wind's blown in'

Nursemaid: nursemaids were almost invariably female. Helen is insulting Geof in the same way Jo did when she compared him to a 'big sister'

the organ grinder . . . the monkey: I expect an answer from the person I am talking to, not from someone else

when the cat's away: this is the first part of the proverb 'When the cat's away, the mice will play'. What Helen implies is that

Jo became pregnant after she and Peter had left to get married

sling your hook: go away. This expression originated in navy slang, before becoming common slang.

can you cut bread on it: Helen is trying to find out how advanced the pregnancy is. If Jo is in her seventh or eighth month, then the bulge caused by her baby would protrude significantly. Helen suggests that the bulge is like a shelf on which to work

communists: communists were not highly regarded in the 1950s in Britain. The Cold War had started and people with communist sympathies were often condemned. Jo wants to annoy Helen by this suggestion

bloody good hiding: severe beating

came a cropper: failed, suffered

pansified little freak: insulting term for a homosexual man

maternity benefit: an allowance which was paid by the government to pregnant women who had worked

bun in the oven: slang expression for 'pregnant'

Lana: Lana Turner was a beautiful Hollywood actress of the 1940s and 1950s. Peter attempts to insult Geof by calling him 'Lana' and later 'Mary', 'Jezebel' and 'Cuddles'

Oedipus: in Greek mythology, Oedipus was the son of Jocasta and Laius, the rulers of Thebes. He did not know who his parents were, and, when he grew up, he killed his father and married his mother. When he realised what he had done, he put out his own eyes. Sigmund Freud used the phrase 'Oedipus Complex' to refer to the conscious or unconscious desire of a male child for his mother. Peter is suggesting that he must have had an Oedipus complex to marry a woman as old as Helen

Jezebel: the wife of Ahab, the king of Israel; sometimes used as a term for a shameless or a scheming woman

Worn out on the beat: exhausted by working as a prostitute

smallest room: euphemism for toilet

went off the deep end: got very angry

fruitcake parcel: homosexual

a box: a coffin

shower: hopeless group of people

here endeth the third lesson: Jo sarcastically compares the advice offered by Helen to the concluding phrase of a reading of a passage from the Bible

Act II, Scene 2

This scene, like Act I, Scene 1 and Act II, Scene 1, opens with music as Jo and Geof dance on to the stage. More time has passed and the time for the baby to be born is very close. The relationship between the couple has deepened. They can talk about anything together, and, although Jo can still be unpredictable, her attachment to Geof is clear. Geof continues his efforts to clean the flat and to make Jo relax by reading. Jo, in an attempt at domestication, has made herself a loose-fitting housecoat, which Geof describes as looking like a shroud. In spite of the banter, they are happy and Geof has the ability to lift Jo's moodiness. Geof is baking a cake, and while they are waiting for it, he moves the couch to clean under it. He finds the dead bulbs that Jo stole from the Park months earlier and had forgotten to plant. The fact that they are dead frightens Jo a little and she asks Geof to hold her hand. He does, and she confides that she had always wanted Helen to hold her hands, but Helen never would. Geof warns her to be careful or she will become exactly like Helen, but Jo refuses to believe him.

As Geof cleans, Jo confesses that she had thought of him as 'interesting' and 'immoral' before she knew him properly, but goes on to tell him that he's 'just like an old woman' in his behaviour. Sensing that she may have hurt him, unintentionally, she asks if he does not like living with her. Geof admits that there are good moments, but adds: 'on the whole it's a pretty trying prospect.' Jo criticises Geof for wearing black shirts, and, when he tells her that he does this for reasons of economy, she reminds him that she earns some money, and adds that few people have the opportunity he has of nursing his 'creative genius'. Jo's 'job' is touching up photographs, and she got that through Geof's kindness.

Jo tells Geof that her mother's father was Irish and that her own father was a mentally-retarded Irishman. Geof, realising that she has been worrying for months about her baby's mental state, reassures her about her father, asking her if it is likely that Helen would have slept with 'a real loony'. Jo confides that she wishes her mother was with her, now that the baby is due, even though she knows they would quarrel. She tells Geof she does not want his college examinations to be ruined by worry, but then adds that it does not matter if he fails since, in this country: 'the more you know the less you earn.' Geof then gives her a present he has bought her, a life-sized baby doll. He hopes that the doll will help Jo come to terms with her own baby. Seeing that it is 'the wrong colour', Jo flings it down and threatens to kill her baby: 'I'll bash its brains out . . . I don't want to be a mother.' Geof offers to go and look for the baby's father and asks if she still loves him. Jo is not certain how much she loved the Boy, who she now names as Jimmie, saying he 'was so tender', and describing how much she wanted company over Christmas, when 'Helen used to go off with some boyfriend or other and leave me all on my own'. Geof wants to know if she remembers when he asked her to marry him. She had gone to lie down on the bed but Geof had not followed her. Jo is glad that it is not 'marrying love' between them, and Geof is content that, for the moment, she needs him. They decide to celebrate with tea and cake, when Helen arrives, laden down with luggage, and carrying a bunch of flowers.

Helen is offered a cup of tea but immediately asks if Jo has anything stronger. She behaves like a solicitous mother, enquiring about Jo's condition and her check-ups. She seems worried when Jo tells her the baby will be born in the flat, reminding her that first babies can cause problems which can be best solved in hospital. Helen starts to make herself at home, picking on Geof and trying to show that she can be of help to Jo. She persuades Geof to leave them alone for a while, and, when he has gone out shopping, she refuses to believe that she was unpleasant to him. Jo tells her: 'You hurt people's feelings and you don't even notice.' Helen shows her the clothes she has bought for the baby and eventually admits she has broken up with Peter. He has gone off with a younger woman, but Helen is philosophical about it. She has managed to save a bit of money, and her time with Peter 'was good while it lasted.' She tries to persuade Jo that she will be needed when the baby is born and when Jo goes back to work, and refuses to accept Jo's word that she and Geof are coping well. Helen changes the subject back to the baby and tells Jo that she has ordered a beautiful cot with 'pink curtains' and 'frills'. Jo shows her the wickerwork cot, which Helen dismisses as being more like a 'laundry basket'. Helen urges Jo to go and lie down, and then turns her attention to the flat, complaining that Jo and Geof have been living 'like pigs in a pigsty'.

While Jo is lying down, Geof returns with Jo's favourite foods. Helen criticises his choice of food, the state of the flat and his choice of cot. Geof gets ready to leave, but as he goes he asks Helen not to frighten Jo with stories about difficult births. Helen refuses to listen to him. She seems horrified when Geof tells her he had planned to be present at the birth. She orders him to leave and take his food with him. He goes for Jo's sake, saying: 'She can't cope with the two of us.' His last comment is on the incomprehensibility of women. He leaves, quietly wishing Jo 'Good-bye . . . and good luck'.

Jo wakes up and asks her mother if there is much pain in childbirth. Helen consoles her, not telling her that Geof has left. For a while, the two women are in harmony, talking about the children singing outside, and about when Helen was a child. Helen is dying for an alcoholic drink but offers to make them both tea, if only she can manage the gas stove. While she is making the tea, Jo tells her that the child might be black. At first, Helen thinks Jo is being morbid, but, when she realises that Jo is serious, she decides to go out 'for a drink'. In her shock, she suggests that Jo drown the baby, let the black midwife adopt it, or put it on the stage and call it 'Blackbird'. When Jo asks Helen if she is coming back, she says 'yes', but there is no guarantee that she will. Jo remembers one of Geof's rhymes and smiles as she sings it.

NOTES AND GLOSSARY:

Little Women: this book, written by Louisa M. Alcott in 1868, is a sentimental account of family life in nineteenth-century America. The book was widely read, especially by young girls, in both Britain and America, because it recounted the growing up of four girls, Meg, Jo, Amy and Beth. It was filmed with June Alyson playing the part of 'Jo'. Jo's reference to the novel suggests that she prefers her literature to be less sentimental. The 'Jo' in *Little Women* suffered one heartbreak before finding her ideal husband. Perhaps Jo realises that she may not be quite so lucky. There is one further theme in *Little Women* which might have made Jo uncomfortable. All the members of the family were extremely loyal to each other. Jo seems to have had little or no experience of loyalty before she met Geof

book barrow: market stall where second-hand books are sold

Edwardian: Edward VII, son of Queen Victoria, reigned from 1901 to 1910. Jo could be saying that Geof is old-fashioned. However, the style of dress worn during Edward's reign became popular with teenage boys in the 1950s. They were called 'Teddy Boys' or 'Teds'

shroud: loose garment put on a dead body

the bulbs: Geof finds dead bulbs under the sofa. They are the ones that Jo stole from the park and planned to plant in Act I, Scene 1

snuff it: slang expression for 'die'

'And he took up his bed and walked': this quotation is from St Mark's Gospel, chapter 2, verse 12. Jesus cured the man who was sick with the palsy: 'And immediately he arose, took up the bed, and went forth before them all'

black shirts: Jo does not like the dark or dark clothes

retouching those bloody photographs: Geof has got Jo a little work which involves using a brush to paint over blemishes on photographs

Irish: Jo excuses her tendency to shout by claiming to be Irish. Later, she tells Geof that her mother's father was Irish. When she uses Irish as an adjective, it means 'comically perverse'

the Battle of Salford Town Hall: Geof's comic remark is based on the suggestion that the Irish often associate themselves with battles, claiming that their ancestors fell in such illustrious battles as Waterloo. Geof suggests that Jo's relatives were mostly from Manchester, and so would not have died in a real battle

Ibsen's *Ghosts*: Henrik Ibsen was a Norwegian dramatist who often dealt with realistic or pessimistic social themes. His play *Ghosts* (1881) deals with the mental problems associated with the disease syphilis

spin me a yarn: tell me a lie

cretin: person with a very low IQ

put away: sent to a mental hospital

loony: slang for 'lunatic'

bin: reduced form of 'loony bin' which is slang for 'mental hospital'

cracked: slang for 'mad, crazy'

you're a cure: you're a tonic; you're good for me

Scoutmaster: homosexuals were often said to favour such roles as scoutmasters, choirmasters and clergymen because they put them in contact with young boys

holds: tight grips used in wrestling

digs: rented accommodation

flitting: northern word for 'moving house'. It sometimes implies 'moving house secretly, without paying one's bills'

all them exercises: this is another of the rare examples when a character is depicted using non-standard grammar. See the section on Language in the Commentary

tricky: difficult, hard to deliver

the Flying Doctor: this is a reference to a popular television series, *The Flying Doctors*, based on the real-life Australian medical service, where doctors fly to emergencies which occur in the Australian outback

district nurse: a nurse who visits people in their homes

barges in: comes in rudely or clumsily

like a bull in a china shop: roughly; breaking things without intending to

make yourself scarce: go out

pansy: homosexual; effeminate man

entitled to keep his child: is legally obliged to pay maintenance to Jo for their child

swanking: ostentatious dress and/or behaviour; showing off

throw-back: person who has the characteristics of our more primitive ancestors

He threw his money about like a man with no arms: he was mean with
his money

put by: saved up

bit of crumpet: attractive, willing girl

midwife: nurse who specialises in delivering babies in a person's own home

etceteras: extras

get: get out

Where would you like those flowers putting?: this is a northern expression equivalent to 'Where do you want me to put the flowers?'

clough: a northern word for 'narrow gorge'

Blackbird: this may be a reference to the popular music hall song: 'If I were a blackbird, I'd whistle and sing,/And follow the ship that my true love sails in,/And on the top rigging, I'd there build my nest,/And pillow my head on his lily-white breast.'

Concluding comments

Whenever we summarise a scene, we automatically highlight some actions and minimise the significance of others. Each one of us will be affected in a unique manner by the characters and by the events, and our responses may differ at different times. Teenagers, for example, will almost certainly identify with Jo and may find that they can sympathise with the boyfriend, Jimmie, or with Geof. Other members of the audience may not fully approve of Helen, but they may understand the difficulties involved in bringing up children, and may have known the urge to run away from problems that seem insurmountable.

We must each read the play for ourselves, and see a performance if that is possible. We must then think about each character, about how the characters interact and influence each other, and about how we are all, to some extent, influenced by circumstances beyond our control. Only when we have done this, will we be in a position to make our own judgments about the quality and value of A Taste of Honey.

Part 3

Commentary

The plot

The details of the plot have been provided in the Summaries of Part 2. Structurally, *A Taste of Honey* is a simple play. It concentrates on the lives of a mother and daughter over a nine-month period. It starts with Jo and her mother alone in a shabby flat and gradually introduces the men. Peter is sexually attracted to Helen and she accepts his interest because he has money and can give her a good time. The Boy and Jo are sexually attracted to each other but their association is based entirely on the physical and is short-lived. The Boy leaves Jo, not knowing and possibly not caring that she is pregnant. Jo establishes a non-physical bond with a young homosexual, Geof, and in it they both find comfort. Peter leaves Helen for a younger woman. Helen returns to Jo and forces Geof to leave Jo and the flat. Helen deserts Jo when she learns that her unborn child may be black. The play ends, as it began, in the shabby flat, now with Jo, entirely alone and going into labour.

Although the play is structurally simple, it is thematically complex. It deals with changing, often conflicting, relationships: the interaction between a mother and a daughter, between a mature woman and a man, between a sexually inexperienced teenager and her lover, and between a pregnant girl and a homosexual boy. It introduces the subjects of prejudice and discrimination, and it raises issues such as the clash between responsibility and the pursuit of personal happiness, the degree of control we have over our lives, and the limited options open to the less privileged members of society.

The play is organised symmetrically. There are two acts, both with two scenes. Act I is slightly shorter than Act II.

   Act I takes up 48% of the play
   Act II takes up 52% of the play

This can be further subdivided:

   Act I, Scene 1 18.5%
   Act I, Scene 2 29.5%
   Act II, Scene 1 29.5%
   Act II, Scene 2 22.5%

There is, however, considerable variation in the scenes, as can be indicated in the following representations of the characters involved in the subdivisions of each scene. It is worth pointing out that only Jo appears alone on the stage, once in Act I, Scene 2 and once at the end of the play.

Act I, Scene 1

H + J   H + J + P   H + P   H + J

Act I, Scene 2

J + B   J + H   J + H + P   J + P   J + H + P   J   J + B

Act II, Scene 1

J + G   J + G   J + G + H   J + G + H + P   J + G

Act II, Scene 2

J + G   J + G + H   J + H   H + G   J + H   J

(H = Helen, J = Jo, P = Peter, B = 'the Boy', G = Geof)

Characters

Every person who sees or reads this play will respond differently to the characters. Teenagers may identify, to different degrees, with Jo, the Boy and Geof. Mothers and daughters may, perhaps, more easily recognise the tensions and rivalry that exist between Helen and Jo. Some may empathise with Helen's desire to get as much pleasure as possible from a life that invariably ends in pain and death. Some may criticise her tendency to run away from problems. And some may think that the male characters are only revealed in so far as they have an impact on the lives of Jo and Helen. Your own view of the five people interacting in *A Taste of Honey* is as valid as anyone else's, as long as you can support your feelings with reference to the text. It is worth stressing, however, that one character's assessment of another may be tinged by love or jealousy or prejudice.

Below, a description of the five characters is provided which you can modify in line with your own response to the play. The five characters can be represented diagrammatically as follows:

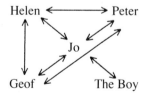

Jo is central, partly because she is the only character to interact with all the others and partly because we increasingly see events and people through her eyes. The older generation is represented by Helen and Peter. Only the Boy is isolated from all the other characters apart from Jo.

Helen

We do not know much about Helen. She mentions her mother who would not have tolerated the rudeness that she herself accepts from Jo (Act I, Scene 1). She does not refer to her father and does not seem to have had a satisfactory relationship with any man. She describes the husband who divorced her as a 'Puritan', suggests that Jo's father was retarded and openly admits that she is interested in marrying Peter because of his money, explaining that 'He's got a wallet full of reasons' (Act I, Scene 1). Peter frequently suggests that she is little better than a prostitute. In Act II, Scene 1, for example, he describes her as 'Worn out on the beat', and Jo accuses her of having had several abortions:

HELEN: I should have got rid of you before you were born.
JO: I wish you had done. You did with plenty of others.

We are given contradictory information about how old Helen is. She admits to being ten years older than Peter, and she seems to confirm Jo's claim that she is forty. Jo, however, is capable of exaggerating. She goes on to say later that Helen is more like 'a sort of well-preserved sixty' than a forty year old, and thinks of Helen as being 'centuries older' than Peter. Indeed it is clear that Jo tries to use the age difference to prise Peter and her mother apart. Whatever age Helen is, she can still look attractive. When she has prepared for an evening out with Peter, he comments that she looks 'utterly fantastic'. The Boy describes her as a 'fancy bit' and admits that he thinks she is beautiful, and even Jo grudgingly acknowledges that she looks 'marvellous' on her wedding day. Delaney may have chosen Helen's name because of Helen of Troy, who was renowned for her beauty.

Helen is intelligent and quick witted. Although she likes a drink, nice clothes and a good time, she can also be kind. She offers to pay for Jo to go to art school, and tells Peter to leave Jo some money when they go away in Act I, Scene 2. She may not have taken much interest in her daughter's welfare, but she does want Jo to learn from the mistakes she has made. Her anger at Jo's pregnancy comes from her own experience of the suffering caused by such an unwelcome event. In fact, in this matter, she shows herself to be more humanitarian than her daughter – when she describes her own story at the time of Jo's birth, and Jo insists that if she had been Helen's husband she would have turned her and the baby out, Helen claims that she would not have behaved so cruelly. However, as with other seemingly straightforward responses from this complex character, there is the suspicion that her motives are not altogether honest. She might not have turned a mother and baby out. She might have walked out herself, as she does when the facts of Jo's pregnancy become too uncomfortable for her to cope with.

Helen seems to have a drink problem. One of the first things she wants when she moves into the flat is a drink. One of the last things she does is to go out for a drink when she learns that her grandchild may be black. She sees her drinking as solace for the suffering of her life: she tells Jo that 'It consoles you'. At the end of Act I, Helen's growing interest in alcohol is commented on by Jo: 'You've emptied more bottles down your throat in the last few weeks than I would have thought possible.' Jo warns that if Helen does not curb her drinking, she could become 'an old down-and-out boozer knocking back the meths.'

Helen is of central significance to the play. She interacts with each of the other characters, apart from the Boy, and her influence on events is strong. Leaving Jo alone in the flat gave her the opportunity to get pregnant. Insulting Geof caused Jo to lose her only friend. She is a complex character, with many contradictions, and in this she is like a real person, not like some theatrical stereotype or stock character. She can be both kind and cruel, understanding and prejudiced, caring and indifferent, sensitive and coarse. She does not work, but likes the pleasures that money can provide. She is not interested in housework or in improving her surroundings beyond a few token gestures to placate Jo. Her reaction to problems is to pretend they do not exist, have a drink, or run away from them.

It is with Geof that Helen reveals the least pleasant side of her nature. She resents the relationship he and Jo share. Perhaps she is jealous of him as Jo was of Peter. Whatever the cause, her viciousness forces Geof out and deprives Jo of the only person who has stood by her.

We do not know whether or not Helen will return to Jo. We must not, however, assume that she has gone for good. If she does return, it may not be out of love or generosity, but out of need. She has broken up with Peter, has no job or close friends that we know of, and may find it easier to return to the flat than to set up home for herself.

Peter

Peter Smith is a car salesman. The stereotype of the crooked second-hand car salesman was not as well established in the 1950s as it is now, but characters like Peter would have contributed to it. Peter, like the other men in the play, tends to be seen through the eyes of the women and so it is not easy to be absolutely objective about him.

As with the other characters in the play, we are not certain about his age. He tells Jo in Act II, Scene 2 that he is ten years younger than Helen, and if Helen is forty, then Peter is thirty. We are also told in Act I, Scene 2 that he lost his eye during the war, when he was a private in the army. A simple calculation, however, suggests that one of these facts may be wrong. If Peter is thirty in 1958, then he was seventeen in 1945 when the war ended and so may not have been in the forces.

He has plenty of money and is willing to spend it. Helen finds this his most attractive characteristic. He has a car, buys a house, spends a lot of time and money in the pub, books tables in restaurants, buys flowers and chocolates, and buys Helen expensive luxuries, such as a fur.

He has a coarse sense of humour and can be racist in his comments. He is selfish. He does not want to share Helen with Jo and he does not care what happens to Jo when he and Helen go off to enjoy themselves. At first, he is infatuated with Helen. He knows she is older than he but he offers her marriage, even though the marriage is unlikely to last. When the marriage fails, Peter finds other women and treats Helen with the contempt that he had earlier reserved for Jo.

Peter can be sentimental, as is shown by his interest in, and knowledge of, popular sentimental songs of the day. He also seems to have social ambitions, perhaps copied from the films from which he has derived his use of 'darling' and his use of slang such as 'Bang-on' for 'excellent'.

Jo

Jo is the central character in the play. She is a teenager, but we are not certain if she is as young as fifteen, the school-leaving age in 1958, or if, as she tells the Boy, she really is 'nearly eighteen'. She may be working class and may have had a poor education, but, like her mother, she is intelligent and articulate. She seems to have artistic talent but she refuses to develop it, preferring to leave school and get a part-time job in a pub.

Jo is eager for affection, but suspicious of it. She rows incessantly with her mother, but Helen may be right when she tells Geof (Act II, Scene 1) that they both enjoy it. She dislikes Peter for taking her mother away but flirts with him, saying, 'Do you fancy me?' and attacks him physically when she does not succeed in annoying him. She agrees to marry a young man she hardly knows, but is aware that their relationship will not last. And although she helps Geof by giving him a place to live, she pries into his personal life and frequently insults his manhood.

Like Helen, she can have swings of mood and dramatic changes of mind. She tells Geof she could not have an abortion, but, when she is depressed, she can cry, 'I'll bash its brains out. I'll kill it', and she certainly makes no practical arrangements for the child's birth. Again like her mother, she is prepared to spend a lot of money on such things as make-up, but, unlike Helen, she seems to have little interest in, or taste for, alcohol.

Jo finds peace and contentment with Geof, but their tendency to seek pleasure in children's rhymes may suggest their youth or an attempt to regain the happiness of childhood that they missed at the time, or indicate that neither of them can cope with the world as it is.

Geof

Geoffrey Ingram is another complex character. He is an art student, and, although it is not made absolutely explicit, he seems to be homosexual. To begin with, he needs Jo because he has been evicted from his lodgings. We are never told *why* he was evicted. Geof says, 'I was behind with the rent', but Jo suggests that his landlady found him with a man.

Geof does not like the squalor that Jo is content to live in. In Act II, Scene 2, he tidies the flat and finds the dead bulbs that Jo forgot to plant. He shows that he is inquisitive and opinionated in Act II, Scene 1, when he discovers Jo's drawings. Like Helen, he sees talent in Jo's art but insists that they are like her, 'sentimental' and 'messy', and lacking in 'design, rhythm or purpose'. Nevertheless, he offers to help provide the discipline she needs, an offer which Jo ignores.

Geof is the only person in the play who loves Jo unselfishly. He tries to help her to earn a little extra money by getting her the job retouching photographs, wants her to look after herself better, and tries to make practical arrangements for the baby's arrival. He offers to marry her, and, although he is not interested in her sexually, he claims, 'I'd sooner be dead than away from you.' It is his love for Jo that persuades him to contact Helen to ask for help, and it is, in part, his love for Jo that persuades him to leave: 'She can't cope with the two of us.'

Geof has to put up with the prying and the insults of Jo, Helen and Peter. At the beginning of Act II, Scene 1, Jo is insensitive and prurient in her desire to find out what men like Geof 'do'. She tells him he is like her 'big sister', and when Helen arrives, Jo orders him to 'buzz off'. Geof hears Helen refer to him as 'a pansified little freak', and although he helps an intoxicated Peter to the bathroom, he has to listen to Peter calling him 'a little fruitcake parcel' and other derogatory names – 'Jezebel', 'Cuddles' and 'Lana'.

The Boy

In Act II, Scene 2, Jo tells Geof that the Boy's name is 'Jimmie'. This is probably correct, although Jo has already told Geof that he was an African prince called Ossini. Naming him 'the Boy' suggests racism. Black men, of all ages and classes, were regularly reduced in status by being referred to as 'boys'. The phrase suggests that the Boy's role as boyfriend is more important than anything else about him. Helen reinforces this view when, in Act II, Scene 1, she accuses Jo: 'You had to throw yourself at the first man you met.' The use of 'the Boy' may also remind the reader of 'Pinkie' in Graham Greene's *Brighton Rock* (1938), who was also introduced as 'the Boy'. But whereas Pinkie is sinister, Jimmie is carefree and gentle.

Jo tells Helen in Act I, Scene 2 that he is twenty-two, that he has worked as a male nurse and is now a sailor doing his national service. He has certainly known prejudice. He admits that Jo is the only girl he has ever met who is genuinely uninterested in his colour, saying, 'You're the first girl I've met who really didn't care.' Like Geof, he dislikes dirt and describes the flat and the surroundings as '. . . the dirtiest place I've ever seen.'

We do not get many insights into his character. Jo describes him as being, like all men, 'only after one thing', and he does not deny that he is only interested in sex. He does not, however, force Jo. Indeed, he takes his lead from her, being willing to stop, or go as far as she will let him. He tells Jo he loves her and asks her to marry him. He probably means what he says at the time. He certainly does not try to mislead Jo. He admits that he is going for a drink with friends in preference to going out with her, and he acknowledges that he is sexually experienced. Despite this greater experience, he is gentle and good-natured towards Jo. We do not see him often in the play, but he is the only character with whom Jo has an uncomplicated, good-humoured relationship.

Similarities between Helen and Jo

Helen and Jo have an uneasy, quarrelsome relationship, yet they have many characteristics in common. Ironically, Jo worries that she may have inherited traits from her father. She has, in fact, inherited most from her mother. They are both:

- intelligent, with an excellent command of the language
- thoughtless
- lacking in any homemaking instinct. The flat is allowed to remain filthy when Helen leaves Jo alone
- talented but unwilling or unable to develop the talent that might have helped them escape
- fatalistic
- interested in their appearance. Jo spends too much of her money on 'stockings and make-up and things'
- lacking in forward planning. They both unintentionally became pregnant
- jealous of people in the other's life: Jo attacks Peter physically, Helen attacks Geof verbally

Language and imagery

Many working-class writers of the 1950s, such as John Braine and Shelagh Delaney, wrote novels and plays which dealt with working-class people. By definition, most of the people on whom these characters were based would have used so-called 'demotic' speech, that is, they would have had regional accents. In Lancashire, many would have dropped the aitches from words such as 'hand' and 'house', and rhymed 'gas' with 'grass' and 'put' with 'but'. They would have employed regional words and expressions such as the exclamation 'Ee!', 'sneck' (door latch) or 'snicket' (alley way), which might not be understood by speakers from other areas. And their speech would normally have contained a number of non-standard features, such as:

(1) multiple negation:
    'I never said nowt to nobody.' (I didn't say anything to anybody.)
(2) 'them' as a demonstrative adjective:
    'Give me them (those) bags.'
(3) 'done', 'seen' rather than 'did' and 'saw' in sentences such as:
    'I done it yesterday.'
    'I seen him last night.'
(4) substitution of 'was' for 'were' and 'were' for 'was' in:
    'I were sat there.'
    'You was tellin' me . . .'
(5) different or no preposition:
    'I'll be here while [i.e. until] six.'
    'Give it me [to me].'
(6) occasional avoidance of the infinitive 'to':
    'What do you want do [to do]?'
(7) 'tha [thou]' and 'thee' as singular pronouns:
    'Tha'll get tha come-uppance!' (You'll get what you deserve.)
(8) 't' instead of 'the':
    'I'd sooner be put on't streets.'

Writers rarely try to represent live speech accurately. They often provide a number of clues to the sort of speech they are representing and leave the rest to the sensitivity of the reader, or, in the case of a play, to the linguistic abilities of the actor. Shelagh Delaney's characters are depicted on the stage as having regional accents, but there are few indications of this in the text. She does not try to show that the boyfriend's Cardiff accent differs from Jo's Manchester speech. Nor does she use many non-standard features of grammar. If she had done so, she might have been commended for the realism of her representation, but this may have distracted attention from the dilemmas her characters face.

In *A Taste of Honey*, Shelagh Delaney, either consciously or unconsciously, has shown that working-class people can be as fluent, articulate and witty as any other group of people represented on the stage. They may not make use of the pointed epigram that was favoured by Oscar Wilde's characters, but they are shown to be intelligent people, capable of commenting shrewdly on life and society. Delaney uses fewer non-standard grammatical features than we might expect, but this is almost certainly deliberate. She wants the audience to laugh *with* her characters, not *at* their use of language, and she also wishes to show that intellectual ability is not dependent on formal education.

There are a number of recurrent images and themes in the play, the most obvious of which are death and decomposition, cars, darkness and dreams. Jo and Helen both raise the subject of death a number of times. In Act I, Scene 1, Jo tells her mother that she had dreamed about her mother's body being dug up. Helen's humorous reaction – 'Well, I've always said that we should be used for manure when we've gone' – turns out to be typical of her. She compares her bed to a coffin, only less comfortable, and she sees death as the only certainty for any of us. This belief makes her determined to 'eat, drink and be merry', causes her lack of respect for '. . . All the pimps, prostitutes and politicians in creation trying to cash in on eternity and their little tin god.'

Jo's attitude to death is the mixture of fascination and horror that is common in teenagers. She dreams about death, or says she does; tells Helen she would rather go to her own funeral than to her mother's wedding; and she responds to Helen's cliché, 'happy the bride that the sun shines on', with: 'Yeah, and happy the corpse that the rain rains on' (Act I, Scene 2).

The image of cars comes up on four main occasions. The Boy carries a toy car in his pocket and he and Jo play with it. Peter is a car salesman and worries that his car will be vandalised when it is parked outside Helen's. Helen uses a car image to illustrate her view that: 'We're all at the steering wheel of our own destiny. Careering along like drunken drivers' (Act I, Scene 1). Jo and Geof talk about cars when Geof comments on the fact that the public has to be bribed by manufacturers to buy their products (Act II, Scene 1), and, in a spontaneous act of imagined generosity, Jo tells him she will buy him a car, or even two, for Christmas.

The third image that recurs in the play is darkness, a darkness that may be physical or mental. Very little action occurs in the light. Helen and Jo move into the flat in the dark. Jo and the Boy meet in the dark of winter and make love in the dark flat. Jo and Geof meet in the summer as night is beginning to fall. Jo tells Helen that she is afraid of the dark, not the outside dark but the darkness that lurks inside buildings. She seems not to care about the darkness of her boyfriend's skin but worries that her child's mind may be affected by the mental darkness that made her father 'retarded'.

Dreams are also thematic in the play. Even in sleep, there is little escape from the certainty of death or from the fears that the unborn child may inherit the problems and inadequacies of its relatives.

Music in *A Taste of Honey*

Music plays several roles in *A Taste of Honey*. A jazz trio is part of the cast and its music opens the play. The individual scenes are split into sections, not by scene changes or drawn curtains, but by the use of music. Characters enter, accompanied by music, and, in the original production by Joan Littlewood, each actor had a theme tune which was played when he or she came on to the stage. All of the characters sing and are linked by their liking for music: jazz, popular ballads and nursery rhymes.

In England, music has been associated with the stage at least as far back as the Middle Ages. In Miracle and Morality Plays, hymns and spiritually uplifting songs were sung. Songs and melodies were also intricately woven into the plot of such Shakespearean plays as *Twelfth Night*. In the sixteenth and seventeenth centuries, masques were popular especially at court. These were often elaborate entertainments, consisting of pantomime, dialogue, dancing and music. Operas and operettas, which often involved a continuous musical structure, gained audiences during the eighteenth and nineteenth centuries, and the works of Sir William Gilbert and Sir Arthur Sullivan widened the appeal of musical dramas still further with such operettas as *H.M.S. Pinafore* (1878) and *The Mikado* (1885). In the 1940s and 1950s, Hollywood films, such as *South Pacific* (1958), popularised musical dramas throughout the English-speaking world. The music in *A Taste of Honey* is thus in the tradition of musical entertainment. The songs and the band serve three clear ends: they give the play some of the variety of music hall entertainment; they link the characters with the popular tunes of the day; and they function like the theme music in a film, highlighting different moods and providing an emotional undercurrent to the action.

Drama as social commentary

First and foremost, a good play must entertain an audience. Often, too, it will treat themes that make us think about people or actions in a new or different way. Jews were not well treated in Elizabethan England, but Shakespeare's Shylock has a dignity and a pathos that must have made an impression on those who saw *The Merchant of Venice* (1596).

A Taste of Honey makes few overt comments on the interests and pre-occupations of the 1950s, but people who saw it or read it might well have asked themselves questions about racism, sexism, prejudice and poverty. This play does not offer solutions, but it and similar productions brought into the public domain issues which many would have preferred to hide. It expressed some of the worries associated with mixed marriages due to the increased immigration from the Caribbean in the 1950s. It raised some of the problems faced by women whose marriages had broken up or who were not content to be tied to the kitchen. It revealed the squalor and poverty in which many inhabitants of inner cities were forced to live, due to inadequate housing and the influx of more and more people into urban areas. It shed light on homosexuality and on the intolerance of most people's attitudes to it. It indicated the growth of a new entrepreneurial class, working class in origin, like Peter, but capable of making large amounts of money, not all of it legally acquired. In short, it focused on one section of the new society emerging in post-war Britain, a section for which traditional values no longer held good.

Concluding remarks

A Taste of Honey is an easy play to comment on because all of us have views on parent–child relationships, love, sex, marriage, alcoholism, abortion, death, desertion and homosexuality. It is not, however, an easy play to classify. Is it a comedy? No, although it has some very funny lines. Is it a tragedy? No, although each character has tragic potential. It is an attempt, by a young playwright, to dramatise people from the same region and the same walk of life as many of the characters in *Coronation Street*. These characters can be witty, clever, kind, coarse, sexist, racist, self-interested and amoral. They are unpredictable, like real people, and that is, perhaps, one of the best compliments one can pay the playwright.

Part 4

Hints for study

Studying *A Taste of Honey*

In studying any play, it is useful to know as much as we can about the period in which it was written, and to be aware of the social conditions in which it was created and in which it was first produced. You should know the text well and be able to offer a short quotation in support of any claims made. You should also try to see characters, not only through the eyes of Jo, but also as they are revealed through their own words and actions. Remember, too, the old adage 'Actions speak louder than words'. If characters think of themselves as tolerant but show by their actions that they are prejudiced, both words and deeds should be taken into account in a full evaluation.

It is also helpful to remember that *A Taste of Honey* is a play which was meant to be watched and enjoyed, and not a philosophical treatise in which every punctuation mark has significance. It will always have its fullest impact on the stage. Nevertheless, there are many advantages in reading a play quietly, methodically and, if possible, at one sitting. In a performance, we may be caught up in the emotional power of the story or swayed by the magnetism of one actor; in a reading, we can be more objective, aware of the strengths and weaknesses of the interlocking personalities, and able to see how the strands in the story are woven into a unique textual experience.

Avoiding the 'anachronistic trap'

When we read a play by Shakespeare or a poem by Milton or a novel by Charlotte Brontë, we are aware that the writers inhabited worlds which, in ways, were very different from our own. We might notice the differences in Shakespeare's language, or the unchallenged certainties of Milton's religious views, or the subservient roles thought appropriate for women in the society of Charlotte Brontë's time. Being aware of such differences helps us to be extra vigilant in our attempts to understand the relevance of the writing, not just to ourselves, but to previous generations.

A play like *A Taste of Honey* may seem to offer few problems to a contemporary viewer or reader. Some of the language, especially slang expressions like 'Bang-on' for 'excellent', may seem dated, but we are not faced with the severe problems of comprehension that a Shakespearean soliloquy can present. We might also miss some of the biblical references in the title and in the repartee, but the amoral world inhabited by Jo, Helen, Peter, Geof and the Boy overlaps the world of the 1990s. And the social constraints do not, at first, seem fundamentally different from those operating today.

It would, however, be anachronistic to expect people living in the 1950s to react as we might to the subjects of colour, homosexuality and children of mixed parentage. Prejudice, of course, is and always has been un-fair. The coarse joke about 'coal black mammies' shared by Peter, Helen and Jo in Act I, Scene 1 is racist and reveals the unattractive side of their characters. Helen's distress on hearing that her grandchild will be black – 'Oh my God! Nothing else can happen to me now. Can you see me wheeling a pram with a . . .' – is a primitive but more comprehen-sible reaction. The mothers of mixed-race children are still often treated harshly. Attitudes in the 1950s were even less tolerant. And the cruel treatment of Geof by Helen, Peter and Jo is, in part, to be explained though not excused by the widely-held belief that homosexuals were criminal perverts. Shelagh Delaney clearly did not agree with such sentiments because she shows Geof to be the least selfish person in the play. Writers like Shelagh Delaney helped to change the prejudices of the 1950s by dramatising them and causing people to discuss them. If we are less prejudiced, it is, in part, due to works like *A Taste of Honey*. The Helens and the Peters and the Jos of the 1950s must be assessed in terms of the social values of their day rather than in terms of ours.

Answering questions on *A Taste of Honey*

There is no set of mechanical rules which a student can follow in order to produce a good answer. However, an answer will have much to recom-mend it if you keep the following points in mind:

(*a*) Read the question paper slowly and select the questions you are best able to deal with. Take your time at this stage, because the results of your examination will depend on the wisdom of your choice. Do not select a question because you happen to see a reference to 'Helen' or 'Geof' or your favourite character. Remember that you know the play well. Select the questions which will allow you to show that knowledge to best advantage.

(*b*) Calculate the amount of time you have for each question and try to keep to a time scheme. If the examination is three hours long and you have four questions to answer, then you should divide your time as follows:

| 10 minutes: | reading the paper and selecting topics |
| 40 minutes: | time allowed for each question |

10 minutes: reading over your paper, checking spelling, punctuation, style and content.

In most examinations, all questions are of equal value, so it would be foolish to lose marks by allowing insufficient time for any question.

(c) If you are producing a project, ensure that it is as neat and as well organised as it can be. Examiners always expect work which is not written under examination conditions to be of a higher standard. Remember to provide a bibliography, that is, a list of all the books you have consulted and found helpful in your research.

(d) Plan your answer in point form before writing your essay or project. If, for example, you are asked to describe and/or comment on the attitudes to love, sex or marriage in the play, you might write down such questions as:

- What do we mean by these terms?
- Are they mutually exclusive?
- What types of love are illustrated? Parental? Filial? Marital? First? Altruistic?
- What sexual relationships are described? Mature? Youthful? Homosexual? Long-term? Frustrated? Satisfactory?
- What marriages are described? Two for Helen, one for Peter, photograph of Peter's brother's wedding, proposal only for Jo.
- Is it possible to decide what the dramatist's views were?

(e) Use quotations wherever possible. This does not mean that you should learn the play by heart. It simply means that an apt quotation, even if it involves only a word or short phrase, reinforces your point. It shows that you know the play, have thought about the issues, and are capable of providing objective evidence in support of your claims.

(f) Answer all parts of the question, but do not give unnecessary information. If, for example, you are asked to compare the characters of Helen and Jo, you must allow equal weight to each character. It would, however, be a waste of time to summarise the plot. A good answer gives not *all* but *only* the information required.

(g) An answer should be written in the form of an essay. An introductory paragraph should examine the topic set for discussion. Each relevant point should then be dealt with in separate paragraphs which make use of complete sentences. Finally, a concluding paragraph should evaluate the topic in the light of your argument and sum up your views on the given subject.

(h) If, in spite of all your good intentions, you find that you have misjudged your time and left only a few minutes to answer your final question, do not panic. It is advisable to write a good opening paragraph, followed by a set of notes showing how your answer would have developed. This alternative is acceptable to most examiners, but a complete set of answers is more acceptable still.

(*i*) Remember that your own style matters. There is no particular merit in long sentences and polysyllabic vocabulary. Keep your writing direct, concise and to the point.

(*j*) Write legibly. There is little point in presenting information if the examiner cannot read your handwriting.

(*k*) Always leave time at the end of an examination to read over your answers and correct any errors, including spelling mistakes.

Topics to think about

The best advice that anyone can be given regarding examination techniques is 'Know your texts well'. If you do, you should be able to answer questions on any topic. The following suggestions, however, should help you think about relevant issues, and discussing them should teach you to express your views clearly and cogently.

(*a*) In order to understand the characters in *A Taste of Honey*, try to perform the following tasks:

- Pretend you are each character in turn
- Try to think about each of your actions
- Explain your actions and make a case for each of them
- What would you change if you had the chance?
- How much freedom of choice did you have?
- Did you think things through or act on impulse?
- What age was each character?
- What advantages are there in our not being absolutely certain what age the main characters are?

(*b*) It has been suggested that the male characters in *A Taste of Honey* are of much less significance than the female characters. Do you agree with the suggestion? Why? List as many reasons as you can for your answer.

(*c*) Try to reconstruct the differences between the 1950s and the present day. Interview your parents or grandparents or neighbours. Try to build up a picture of the period by asking them such questions as:

- Who was the Prime Minister in 1958?
- What were the problems facing the country in the 1950s?
- How extensive was home ownership in the 1950s?

- When did immigration from the West Indies and Asia begin? Why?
- What songs were popular in the period?
- What films were popular?
- How many families had television sets? What programmes were popular?
- How much did common items cost? a daily paper? a loaf? a pint of milk? a gallon of petrol? a glass of beer? a bus ride to work? a car?
- What did people think about children born outside marriage? About mixed marriages? About homosexuals? About divorce?

(d) Consider the different love relationships in *A Taste of Honey*, namely:

- Jo and Helen
- Jo and the Boy
- Jo and Geof
- Helen and Peter

Describe each from the point of view of the different partners. Try to answer some or all of the following questions and pose some of your own:

- Do Jo and Helen love each other? Are they simply stuck with each other?
- Does the Boy love Jo? How do you know?
- Does Jo love the Boy? Does she expect that they might live 'happily ever after'?
- What are the reasons for Geof's kindness to Jo? Could you call it 'love'? Why?
- Can you explain Peter's interest in Helen? Is it purely physical?
- Does Helen love or even like Peter? What do they have in common? A love of life? A love of a good time? A liking for popular songs? Animal passion?

(e) The play deals with a number of so-called 'taboo' themes such as death and decomposition. Which characters are most obviously associated with these themes? How do they deal with them? It is difficult to talk simply and directly about death and decomposition. Why? Why does Shelagh Delaney feel that they are suitable topics for a play? Make a list of some of the expressions used to avoid the straightforward 'he died', expressions such as:

- he passed on
- he went to his eternal reward
- he kicked the bucket
- he popped his clogs

The first two are euphemisms, the second two humorous clichés. How do the characters in the play refer to death? Why?

(*f*) Can you describe the prevailing mood of the play? Is it pessimistic? comic? realistic? fatalistic? cruel? kind? a mixture? Which characters are most closely associated with the different adjectives used above? Select six adjectives to describe each character. Have you used the same adjectives for any two? Why? Can you change them? Have you improved your description of the character?

(*g*) How realistic is the plot of *A Taste of Honey*? Write down the various strands. Which of them seem plausible? implausible? Does the combination of events strain your credulity? Why? Do you agree that truth can be stranger than fiction? Does it matter if a play appears realistic or not?

(*h*) The ending of *A Taste of Honey* is inconclusive. We do not know what happens to Jo and her baby. We do not know whether or not Helen returns. We do not know whether or not Geof returns. We do not know if Jo ever sees the Boy again. Try writing your own conclusion to the play. When you have done so, decide what dramatic advantages there are in *not* knowing what happens.

(*i*) Suppose you were invited to put on a production of *A Taste of Honey*. Answer the following questions and pose some of your own.
- What sort of set would you use? Why? How would you create the appearance of shabbiness and dirt? Would the appearance reflect on the characters?
- Which character would you cast first? Why?
- What colour would Helen's hair be? Why? Are blonde characters stereotyped?
- Would Peter have a moustache? Would he sleek his hair down?
- Would the Boy wear his uniform?
- How would you dress Jo? Geof?
- If you gave each character a signature tune, what would each be? Why? What dramatic advantages might there be in giving each character such a tune?
- Would you develop the humour in the play? How?
- Would you produce the play as if it were taking place in the 1950s or today? If you decide that you would produce the play as if it were taking place today, how would you bring it up to date?

Specimen questions and suggested answers

It is neither useful nor desirable to offer students a set of 'model' answers without first explaining a number of points.

(1) Such answers are meant to be *guides* to essay-writing techniques. They should be read, thought about and re-read, as one individual's response to a topic. They are not intended to be learnt by heart or considered the final word on any subject.

(2) Students who rely too heavily on 'model' answers are unlikely to use their own knowledge creatively. It is important to remember that many questions will elicit the use of the same material, but each question will require a unique selection and organisation. No model answer, however good, can be used for more than one question, although the techniques used will apply more widely.

(3) Throughout these notes, we have tried to offer ideas and suggestions rather than to claim that there is only one possible interpretation of any episode or action. Students are encouraged to evaluate the data, to think about what others have said, but to make up their own minds about characters, relationships and events.

It may, however, be useful to indicate how a student should deal with an examination-type question, and so we provide two essay questions, one appropriate answer and a suggested plan for the second.

Question 1: '*A Taste of Honey* is obviously the work of a young writer. It lacks clearly delineated characters and it fails to tell a coherent story.' Discuss.

Plan INTRODUCTION:
  (a) In what ways can the play be considered the work of a young writer?
  (b) Are the characters inadequately delineated?
  (c) Does it fail to tell a coherent story?

BODY OF ESSAY:
Each question raised in the introduction dealt with in full.

CONCLUSION:
The play may well be the work of a young writer, but the two criticisms do not necessarily follow from that fact and, indeed, some of the intrinsic originality may be associated with the playwright's youth.

Essay answer
Shelagh Delaney was eighteen when *A Taste of Honey* was first produced in London. It is, therefore, undoubtedly true that the play is the work of a young writer. Being so young may well have had disadvantages. Her experience of life was, inevitably, limited, and her experience of the theatre probably even more so. By the time she was eighteen, she would

have seen only a small number of plays on the stage and on television, although the large number of films she watched would, to some extent, have compensated for this lack. To admit that she was young and inexperienced, however, does not automatically imply that her characters are inadequately delineated or that she was at that age incapable of telling a coherent story. Many mature writers may fail to breathe life into their characters or to convince an audience of the coherence of their narrative. Delaney's characters may not be easy to pigeonhole and her story may not have the sequenced development we find in detective stories, but both characters and story have something better: they have the naturalness and apparent aimlessness often found in life.

There have been many young actors and actresses, young musicians and performers in the British theatre, but very few playwrights have had successful London productions even in their twenties. Delaney's play is, from this point of view, unique. It may not be as polished or as witty as Oscar Wilde's *The Importance of Being Earnest* or as thought-provoking as Beckett's *Waiting for Godot*, but it has the originality of a writer creating her own style.

The critic who claimed that Delaney's characters were not clearly delineated was probably influenced by the number of things we do not know about them. We do not know, for example, how old Helen is, why she seems incapable of having a satisfactory relationship with a man, why she runs away from problems, or why she can swing from gentleness and generosity to cruel indifference. We are never told how or when Jo met the Boy, why she decides to sleep with him, or even whether they really think they loved each other. Indeed, we cannot be certain of the relationships between Jo and any of the characters with whom she interacts. Does she love or hate her mother? Perhaps both. Is she jealous of Peter for taking her mother away, or jealous of Helen for being attractive to men? Does she simply drift into her affair with the Boy out of loneliness, or is she trying to prove that she can be independent of Helen? And her relationship with Geof is perhaps most enigmatic of all. She seems to love him, but she hurts him and allows others to be hurtful to him. She needs him, but it is not clear if her need is temporary or permanent.

When we list such problems or think in abstract terms about a play about a 'semi-whore', a pregnant teenager, an ageing Romeo with an eye-patch, a Black lover and a homosexual friend, we can understand why *A Taste of Honey* might be criticised. But such lists fail to take into account two important facts. Delaney's characters are like real human beings in that they live in our memories long after the play is over. And secondly, only stereotyped characters can be fully described and explained.

The final part of the criticism is that *A Taste of Honey* fails to tell a coherent story. It certainly tells a series of interlocking narratives: Helen's affair with Peter, Jo's affair with the Boy, the love-hate relationship between Helen and Jo, and the development of a friendship between a pregnant girl and a homosexual boy. As with the characters, however, the story is not sharply and incontrovertibly fixed. It does not progress from A to B and B to C with the inevitability of a telephone book. As in real life, episodes occur which do not contribute to an overarching plan, and characters do not always behave as we might like them to.

There is truth in all three elements of the criticism highlighted in this question. *A Taste of Honey* is undoubtedly the work of a young writer, and it is not difficult to find problems with both characters and plot. Delaney was one of the youngest playwrights to have her work produced in London, but her youth was potentially a strength as well as a weakness. She was original in her attitude to both characters and story, and was prepared to include the controversial topics that would have occupied the minds of young people in the late 1950s. The play may lack the subtlety and polish to be found in the works of some older contemporaries, but Delaney suffuses her characters and her story with vigour and vitality, and these qualities are more enduring than any preconceived notions of appropriateness.

Question 2: To what extent could *A Taste of Honey* be described as 'a kitchen sink drama'?

Plan INTRODUCTION:

In what ways can the play be considered a 'kitchen sink drama'?

The label 'kitchen sink drama' is often applied to a play which has some or all of the following characteristics:

- it is set in a working-class environment, often in a flat or bed-sitter in an urban area
- it deals with domestic issues
- it deals with the conflicts that can arise between people who are poor and are living in cramped conditions
- it uses ordinary, everyday language in an attempt to provide the audience with an accurate picture of one section of society

BODY OF ESSAY:

Paragraph 1: Describe briefly the setting of *A Taste of Honey*. The scenes are mostly in a dingy bed-sitter in Salford, Manchester, where there is little heating, a shared bathroom and where the view from the window includes the gasworks. Peter and Geof, in particular, are horrified by the dirt and the cockroaches.

Paragraph 2: Give a short description of the domestic issues dealt with in the play: relationships between mother and daughter
between mother and boyfriend, Peter
between Jo and Peter

between Jo and the Boy and Geof
between Helen and Peter and Geof

Paragraph 3: Short account of the types of conflict described in the play and the reasons for them.

Paragraph 4: Comment on the use of language. Although *A Taste of Honey* uses the grammar of Standard English, it has the colloquial vigour of ordinary, everyday language.

CONCLUSION:

The conclusion should include such points as the following:

A Taste of Honey certainly has many of the characteristics associated with the 'kitchen sink' genre, but such a label does not do justice to the scope of Delaney's play. Delaney creates a working-class world where there is little time for idealism or sentimentality. It is a world where people daily face problems and difficulties and where, occasionally, they can transcend their dilemmas.

It can be partially described by several labels, such as 'angry', 'working-class', 'gritty', 'defiant', 'comic', 'potentially tragic', 'socially aware', but, like most good plays, no single label can capture its variety and scope.

Part 5

Suggestions for further reading

IN ORDER to appreciate the originality and power of *A Taste of Honey* it would be helpful to have read some or all of the following plays that were first written or produced in England in the 1950s.

BECKETT, SAMUEL: *Waiting for Godot*, Faber and Faber, London, 1956.
BEHAN, BRENDAN: *The Quare Fellow*, Methuen, London, 1956.
——: *The Hostage*, Methuen, London, 1958.
OSBORNE, JOHN: *Look Back in Anger*, Faber and Faber, London, 1956.
PINTER, HAROLD: *The Birthday Party*, Methuen, London, 1958.

In addition, Shelagh Delaney's style and preoccupations can be explored by reading her short stories, *Sweetly Sings the Donkey* (1963), her other plays, including *The Lion in Love* (1960), *Did Your Nanny Come from Bergen?* (1970) and *Don't Worry about Matilda* (1981), and the screenplays she wrote for such films as *Charlie Bubbles* (1968) and *Dance With a Stranger* (1982).

Students wishing to examine criticism that provides useful information about the play and the period in which it was written should read some or all of the following:

ALLSOPP, KENNETH: *The Angry Decade*, Peter Owen, London, 1958.
BANHAM, MARTIN: *The Cambridge Guide to World Theatre*, Cambridge University Press, Cambridge, 1988.
GOORNEY, HOWARD: *The Theatre Workshop Story*, Eyre Methuen, London, 1981.
HINCHLIFFE, ARNOLD P.: *British Theatre 1950–70*, Basil Blackwell, Oxford, 1974.
KITCHIN, LAURENCE: *Mid-Century Drama*, Faber and Faber, London, 1962.
LEWIS, PETER: *The Fifties*, Heinemann, London, 1978.

When you have studied the play and read some literary criticism, try to see some films from the 1950s, such as *The Wild One* (1954), starring Marlon Brando, and *Rebel Without a Cause* (1955) with James Dean. Try to assess how such films may have influenced the writing of Shelagh Delaney.

The author of these notes

LORETO TODD is Reader in International English at the University of Leeds. Educated in Northern Ireland and England, she has degrees in English Language, Literature and Linguistics. Dr Todd has taught in England and in West Africa, and has lectured in Australia, Canada, the Caribbean, Europe, Papua New Guinea, Singapore and the United States of America. She has published twenty books, including *International English Usage* (1990), *Variety in Contemporary English* (1991) and *Mediaspeak* (1992). At present, she is engaged in a study of the language of literature.